BELWIN MASTER SOLOS

F L U T E E A S Y

GRADED SOLOS for the Developing Musician
Edited by KEITH SNELL

CONTENTS

ORIENTATION

This book is one of three levels of flute solos in the Belwin Master Solos series. Prepared under the direction of Keith Snell, each of these folios contains a collection of graded solos that should prove to be a useful source for both the student and the teacher of the flute.

Each folio will contain works from the Renaissance, Baroque and Classical periods, folk songs and traditional tunes, and a selection of original compositions for flute. For the student, these solos will provide material with specific challenges in rhythm, range, and key signatures in music that is both instructive and enjoyable to perform. The teacher will find these solos useful because each has been selected and arranged to challenge the student in different areas of technique and musicianship while providing exposure to a variety of musical styles that are enjoyable to perform. In addition, special attention has been given to creating accompaniments that are easy to play yet at the same time add interest to the solo parts.

EASY LEVEL - SOLOS

The solos in this folio are designed to provide limited challenges to the beginning flute student in range, key signatures and rhythms, and in the technique of solo performance.

The pieces have been arranged so that each will focus on one or two areas of development at a time in order to not overload the student with too many challenges at once. In the area of meters, only the basic duple and triple quarter note meters have been used. Subdivided meters are dealt with in the intermediate and advanced levels of the Belwin Master Solos for Flute. Key signatures have been limited to two sharps or flats; however, in some pieces, closely related keys are briefly explored through the use of accidentals. Since the establishment of good rhythm is a fundamental part of every beginning player's technique, the rhythms in this volume have been kept very simple. Dotted rhythms have been limited to quarter and half notes and have been kept to a minimum. Syncopations and tied rhythms are explored in the intermediate and advanced levels.

In an effort to expose the beginning student to a cross section of musical styles, arrangements of music from the various stylistic periods have been included. In order to accommodate the restrictions of key, meter and rhythm previously discussed, it has been necessary to make alterations to the original form of some of the pieces. However, this has permitted the inclusion of many pieces which would not normally be considered playable by the beginning student. It is hoped that by being introduced to these musical styles at such an early stage, students will develop an interest and appreciation for these styles and will be encouraged to explore them further as their technique develops.

Burlesque

Leopold Mozart (1719-1787)
Arranged by Chris Nolan

Jeanetta Waltz

Doc Barber

Three Chinese Folk Songs
1. Song of Hoe

Traditional
Arranged by Keith Snell

2. The Filial Crow

Traditional
Arranged by Keith Snell

3. Ballad of the Yellow Sun

Traditional
Arranged by Keith Snell

Rondo

Keith Snell

Bourée

Georg Philipp Telemann (1681-1767)
Arranged by Keith Snell

Elegy

John Tyndall

Night Song

Derek Haydn

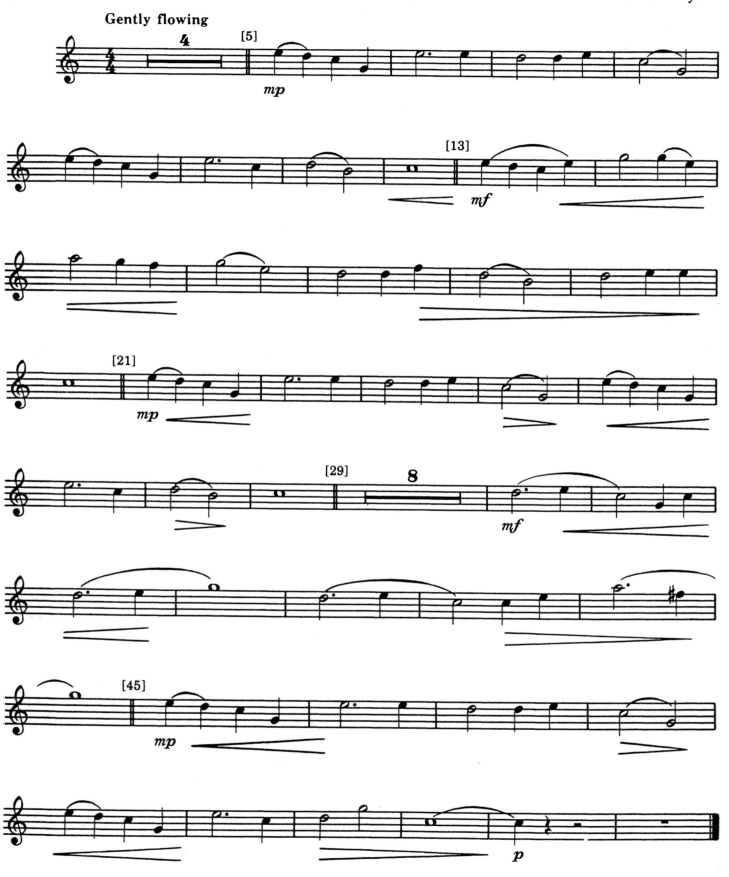

Processional

Louis Claude Daquin (1694-1772)
Arranged by John Tyndall

Rigaudon

Georg Böhm (1661-1733)
Arranged by Keith Snell

Sarabande

Daniel Speer (C. 1625-?)
Arranged by Keith Snell

The Pedlar

Russian Folk Song
Traditional
Arranged by Keith Snell